Billy
the Thrush

Written by Jillian Sullivan
Illustrated by Peter Bray

PEARSON

When Mum got sick, I would sit after school with my back against the old plum tree next to the shed. From there, I could watch when the neighbours came over with pots of soup for us and I could see Mum's face light up when she opened the door and saw them.

I just stayed where I was – happy to sit with the quiet of the tree for company and look at the things around me, such as old plum stones, brown and damp, and an empty snail shell that glinted like a tortoiseshell jewel in the sun. That's how come I happened to be there when I heard a bird crying out as if in distress.

Following the sounds of the bird cries, I searched
in the fallen leaves and around the edge of a hay
bale. Finally, in the doorway of the old shed,
I saw it … a baby bird: no nest or parent birds, no
brothers or sisters. It was just a speckled clump of
feathers with hooded eyes and a wide-stretched beak.

My fingers folded over the wings and I lifted the bird
to my chest. "I'll keep you safe," I promised as
I stood there under the branches of the plum tree.

The only thing I knew about babies was that mum was having one and that was why she got sick at times and couldn't cook our dinner. But I did know I would have to find a safe place for the baby bird because next door was a big ginger tomcat – swaggering and yowling and forever hungry for small living things.

I took the bird into the shed and made a nest with an old tee shirt inside a seed box. Pulling the shed door shut, I clambered around the side of the shed and over the stacked seed trays, looking for cat-sized holes. But the shed was as solid as a fortress. My baby thrush would be safe.

When I went back into the shed, the tiny bird was huddled into the tee shirt but it screeched with hunger when it saw me. I went out to the compost heap with a long twig, and poking down found some small, wriggly worms.

Quickly I carried the worms back in a cupped hand to the bird.
They went down in a gulp. I went out to the garden again and
brought back more worms.

Now the bird was quiet and shut its eyes.
I laid my finger gently on its fragile body
and feathers. It looked like a baby
thrush. I thought of how it had
fallen – from the tree world of
its nest into danger.

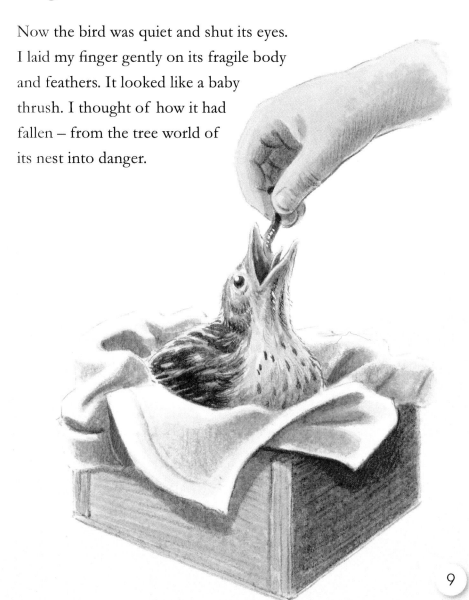

Every day after school, I rushed home. I didn't have time to sit about anymore. I was a full-time dirt-searcher, stick-poker, branch-turner. I found worms in the grass, between the lettuces and under the rotten pumpkin left over from last winter. When I came through the shed door, the baby thrush eyed me with shiny black eyes, beak wide and calling. Afterwards, even fatter, it would sit in the cup of my hand.

I told Mum about my baby bird. "Is it strong and healthy?" Mum asked from her pillow.

"Yes I think so," I said. "It's really hungry. I have to find so many worms!"

Every night, I gave Mum a progress report. Sometimes I would ask her things, such as "When do birds fly?"

"When they can," Mum said.

Sometimes we talked about the baby. "When's the baby coming?"

"Only the baby knows," said Mum.

"It's like a bird in a shell, waiting to hatch," I said.

At the weekend the wind blustered and blew ferociously at the house all night. When I ran outside for the early morning worms, I saw, with a terrible lurch in my stomach, the door to the shed was open. Then I heard a crash.

I ran towards the door. Out of the shed leapt the yowling ginger tom. Inside the shed, the seed box nest was bare.

But there, under the table in the dirt, was my bird. The little thrush was cold. It trembled in my hand. I put it in my chest pocket next to my own thumping heart and sat on the upturned wheelbarrow in the sun.

Revived by the warmth of the sun, skin, cotton and beating heart, the little bird peeped out again. Up in the sky, a thrush flew past and landed in the plum tree.

When I took the baby thrush back to the shed, I closed the door with a big loop of wire.

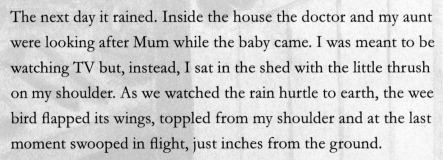

The next day it rained. Inside the house the doctor and my aunt were looking after Mum while the baby came. I was meant to be watching TV but, instead, I sat in the shed with the little thrush on my shoulder. As we watched the rain hurtle to earth, the wee bird flapped its wings, toppled from my shoulder and at the last moment swooped in flight, just inches from the ground.

My baby thrush flew!

I ran out into the rain with my arms out wide. The rain running down my face turned my grey tee shirt black. I was out there, full of flight, when my aunt came out the door to call me.

I had a brother, a baby brother, with hair wet like new feathers and a searching hungry mouth. A brother that would one day be ready to run like me, to taste rain, feel the sun and some day, maybe, see my thrush flying free.

Recounts

Recounts tell a story. A character from the story called a narrator tells the story from their point of view.

How to Write a Recount

Step One

Decide on a storyline.

Your storyline should have:

An Introduction that quickly tells the readers:

- Who the story is about (the characters)
- Where and when the story happened (the setting).

Remember

Use the first person: I, we, me...

Step Two

Think about the main **characters** and describe what they look like and how you imagine they might think, act and feel.

Billy

- a ten-year-old boy
- likes sitting under the plum tree
- kind
- caring
- responsible
- determined

Mum

- a 30-year-old woman
- expecting a baby
- sometimes feels unwell and doesn't like to cook
- likes to hear about the baby bird

Step Three

Think about the **setting**.

Where did the events happen?
What might the characters

see   **hear**   **feel**   **smell**   **or taste?**

Step Four

Think about the **events** in order of sequence.

Guide Notes

Title: **Billy and the Thrush**

Stage: Advanced Fluency

Text Form: Recount

Approach: Guided Reading

Processes: Thinking Critically, Exploring Language, Processing Information

Written and Visual Focus: Illustrative Text

THINKING CRITICALLY
(sample questions)
- Look at pages 2-3. What do you think might happen in this story?
- What inferences can you make about why the narrator was "happy to sit with the quiet of the tree for company"?
- What is meant by the term "quiet of the tree"?
- Look at pages 4-5. Why do you think the author emphasised the baby bird had "no nest or parent birds, no brothers or sisters"?
- Look at pages 6-7. How can you tell the narrator took his promise to keep the little bird safe seriously?
- Look at pages 8-9. What inferences can you make about the narrator's character so far?
- Look at pages 10-11. Why do you think the author introduced Mum and the coming baby to the story? What do you think is the purpose for this?
- Look at pages 12-13. Billy felt a terrible lurch in his stomach when he saw the open shed door and the cat. How do you think the author wanted the reader to feel about this event?
- Look at pages 14-15. Why do you think the author emphasised the text "My baby thrush fle\
- Look at pages 16-17. Why do you think Billy compared his new baby brother to the baby thrush? What links or parallels does he make?
- Throughout the story, Billy is always alone except for Mum. What inferences can you make from this?
- What questions do you have about this text?
- Why do you think the author wrote the story?

EXPLORING LANGUAGE
Vocabulary
Clarify: company, tortoiseshell, distress, hooded eyes, swaggering, clambered, compost heap, fragile, lurch

Synonyms: Discuss synonyms for *fragile, healthy, revived*

Antonyms: Discuss antonyms for *quiet, fragile, healthy*

Similes: *like a tortoiseshell jewel, as solid as a fortress*

Alliterations: *blustered and blew, full of flight*